shawn johnson
OLYMPIC CHAMPION

STORIES BEHIND THE SMILE

shawn johnson
OLYMPIC CHAMPION

STORIES BEHIND THE SMILE

LEXICON

DES MOINES

Thank you

To the ones who got me to where I am today...

My **COACHES** who believed in me, pushed me, and challenged me to become the best gymnast I could be. You always allowed me to have fun and made sure I was doing it for myself. You became like parents to me and will always be. Thank you so much for everything you've done. **Through it all I've wanted to make you both proud.**

My **TEAMMATES** who supported me through every decision, became my biggest group of cheerleaders, and went through countless hours of squat jumps and handstands right next to me so I wouldn't have to do them alone. **I couldn't have made it this far without you being the greatest team players and my best friends.**

My **SPONSORS** for helping me expand my career and tell my story. **You are amazing and so much fun to work with.** You took me in and became so close that it no longer feels like business but like family.

My incredible **AGENT** who has helped me become someone I only dreamed of becoming. **You have opened up so many opportunities and helped me experience things I will never forget.** You have become part of the Johnson family and always will be. I am lucky to be able to work with you.

My best friend and cousin, **TORI**, who has been by my side from the beginning. **You're just like my sister and I couldn't have done it without you.** You have attended almost every meet I've ever competed in. The one I remember the most is my elite qualifier. You were the first one I ran to after the results came in. You had the perfect shoulder to shed my tears of joy on. **You're my world, my family, and my inspiration.** I hope you know that.

Most importantly—my **PARENTS.** I feel as if there aren't even words to express how I feel. We have been through so much this past year that we haven't really even had time to enjoy each other's company or give the proper reward to everything that's happened. I know, as an only child, it was harder than ever imaginable for you to sit back and watch as your little girl took to the largest stage and cleared the biggest obstacles alone. I don't know if there is anything I could ever do to repay you for everything you've done. **You are my life and have been so supportive through it all.** You never pushed me to become a better gymnast or an Olympian, but to be a better person. You always believed that was more important than any title, and because of that I've been able to stay the same Shawn Johnson I've always been. **I will forever be your little girl and I just hope you know how much I love you.**

And to my **FANS**—a big thank you for supporting me! **Dream Big, Have Fun, and Follow Your Heart...**

— Shawn —

I JUST FEEL LIKE SOMEONE WHO'S WORKED
HARD AND SEEN HER DREAMS COME TRUE.
I DON'T SEE MYSELF AS A CELEBRITY AT ALL.
I NEVER EXPECTED THINGS
TO GET THIS FAR OR THIS BRIGHT.

Published by
Lexicon
A division of Lexicon Consulting, Inc.
300 East Locust, Suite 230
Des Moines, Iowa 50309
www.lexiconconsultinginc.com

Copyright © 2008 Lexicon

Director of Brand Management, Book Marketing &
Sales: Eyecon Brand Management

Unless otherwise credited, all images are courtesy
of Shawn Johnson.

Cover image © Getty Images

ISBN 978-1-934417-01-0

Book Design by Lexicon
Cover Design by Lexicon

Printed in the United States of America
2008

CONTENTS

GROWING
up
1

My parents, Doug and Teri, are one of the main reasons I am where I am today. They met and **fell in love in high school,** got married in 1977, and had me 15 years later. The three of us have always been really close. **My mom and dad are my biggest supporters and my biggest fans.** They've always been there for me, and I know they always will be.

THEY'RE JUST THE
MOST NORMAL PARENTS
THERE ARE.

THEY NEVER PUSHED ME
TO DO ANYTHING I DIDN'T WANT TO DO.

MY PARENTS THINK
IT'S **MANDATORY**
THAT I LEAD A
NORMAL LIFE.

I CAN'T IMAGINE

GROWING UP WITHOUT MY TWO GOLDEN RETRIEVERS, *Dude and Tucker.*

My parents had Dude before I was born, and when he passed away we got Tucker. **I love them both.**

They're the best friends a girl could ask for.

IN MY FAMILY, I'm the baby of my generation.

As a result, my mom says I've always been kind of impish and spoiled with most of my cousins, who are in their 20s and 30s now. **I got away with a lot more than I probably should have,** but everyone was really playful with me. Mom tells me we'd all go out for dinner and I'd be under the table TYING EVERYONE'S SHOES TOGETHER.

Me with my family, **the people** *I love the most.*

> ## SHE GOT THE SHORT GENES FROM US,
> AND THE DOCTOR SAID SHE PROBABLY WOULDN'T GROW ANYMORE.
>
> —Doug

I'm especially close to **my cousin, Tori.** We practically grew up together, and **she's always been like a sister to me.**

IN MANY RESPECTS I WAS A
NORMAL LITTLE GIRL.

BUT...

...I SKIPPED CRAWLING AND STARTED WALKING AT **9 MONTHS.** I EVEN DID PULL-UPS ON MY PLAYPEN. THAT'S WHY **GYMNASTICS IS SO PERFECT FOR ME.**

"SHAWN WAS ALWAYS FULL OF A LOT OF STUFF SHE SHOULDN'T BE FULL OF. AND **SHE WAS JUST INCREDIBLY PHYSICAL**—THAT'S WHY WE PUT HER IN GYMNASTICS. SHE WAS ALWAYS ON THE GO, CLIMBING AND RUNNING— AND **SHE ALWAYS HAD A HUGE GRIN ON HER FACE.** SHE WAS SO FULL OF ENERGY AND WAS JUST A **HAPPY KID.**"

—TERI

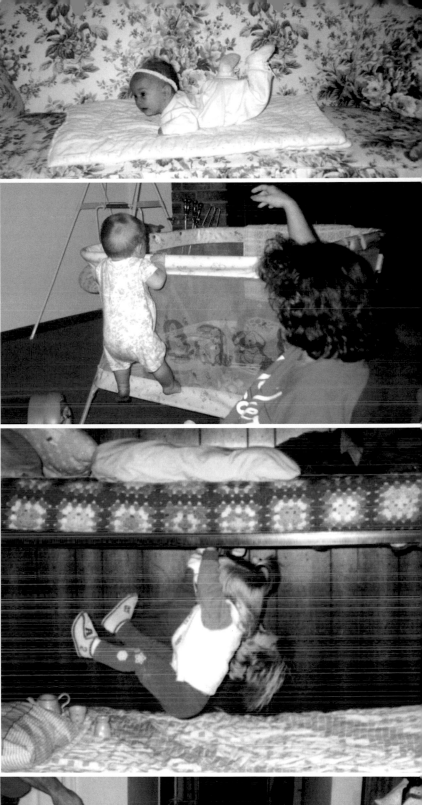

"We had an **ELITE ATHLETE** living in our home

AND WE DIDN'T DO ANYTHING SPECIAL

FOR HER."

—Doug

"Doug and I never made Shawn's gymnastics so important that it wouldn't allow for other things in her life. **We let her do anything other normal kids would do,** but we've done it in a way that balances with her training. I NEVER WANTED SHAWN TO FEEL LIKE SHE WAS A PRISONER OF GYMNASTICS.

SHAWN'S SUCCESS JUST HAPPENED without us putting a lot of effort into it. There are parents out there that work so hard to get their kids to that level, but we never did. **We didn't follow through at home like you are supposed to.** We didn't make her work out at home. She never practiced at home. I never wanted a piece of equipment in my home; I didn't want the responsibility. WHEN SHE LEFT PRACTICE, I WANTED HER TO MYSELF."

—Teri

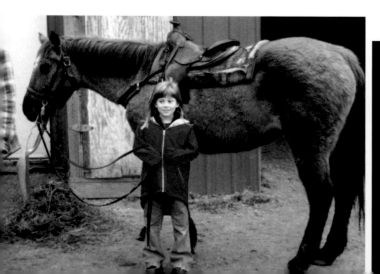

IF I HAD AN **ENTIRE DAY TO MYSELF** and couldn't do anything gymnastics-related, I'd like to do the whole **SPA EXPERIENCE.** Or, if I was feeling adventurous, I'd try **rock climbing, skydiving, skiing,** or horseback riding.

"Shawn is awfully stubborn and strong-willed now that she's a teenager. **She's really independent,** which I want her to be. I think that's because of gymnastics. It breeds an "I can take care of myself" attitude because she has to be so responsible.

She needs to learn things the hard way, which I don't think is a bad thing. When she first got her driver's license, I don't know how many times I would say, "Honey, you need to slow down. You're driving too fast." I remember thinking, "I hope she gets a ticket because she's not listening." Well, she got a ticket, and now she slows down! I'm glad she got it.

Shawn wants to be a good kid. I hate that she has to learn things the hard way, but I think it's good for her to learn that she's not above rules and regulations, and that **she's got opportunities available to her that many kids don't.** It helps keep her from becoming arrogant and taking advantage of the life she's got open to her.

GYMNASTICS HAS MADE HER **INCREDIBLY SELF-CONFIDENT** AND **MORE** MATURE THAN SHE REALLY NEEDS TO BE RIGHT NOW. BUT EVERYTHING SHAWN HAS GOTTEN BACK FROM THIS HAS BEEN POSITIVE, AND **I WOULDN'T TAKE ANYTHING BACK.** I WOULDN'T ENCOURAGE OTHER PEOPLE TO DO IT UNLESS THEY REALIZE WHAT THEY ARE GIVING UP. I WOULD GIVE ANYTHING TO HAVE ALL THOSE YEARS OF HER LIFE BACK. **BUT IT'S GOOD.**

—TERI

Just like any other teenager, I have rules. My curfew depends on what I'm doing the next day. On weekends, **the latest is midnight.** On school nights, it's 9:30.

I'm also expected to keep my room tidy. I keep my room clean when I don't have luggage everywhere. When I first get home from traveling, I'm so overwhelmed and everything is everywhere. But when I don't have that much stuff, **I'm very organized.**

2

BEING

shawn

MY FAVORITES

PLACE TO TRAVEL

HAWAII

COLOR

turquoise

BOOK

The Eight by Katherine Neville
(Ballantine Books, 1997);
You Go Girl! Winning the Woman's Way
by Kim Doren and Charlie Jones
(Andrews McMeel Publishing, 2000)

ANIMAL

DOG (GOLDEN RETRIEVER)

ICE CREAM FLAVOR

vanilla **or** strawberry
cheesecake

CELEBRITY

LANCE ARMSTRONG

SONG

"Something Special"
by Colbie Caillat (Beijing Olympic Mix
from AT&T Team USA Soundtrack)

HOMETOWN HANGOUT

appare japanese steakhouse

FOODS

sushi; strawberries

DRINK

COCA-COLA in a glass *bottle*

BAND

Rascal Flatts

© JAMES A. STEPP - LEXICON   © JAMES A. STEPP - LEXICON

Your life is going to change. HIGH SCHOOL'S TOUGH, ESPECIALLY WHEN YOU'RE A LITTLE BIT DIFFERENT. But it makes you a little bit tougher and you get through it. —SHANNON MILLER, OLYMPIC AND WORLD GYMNASTICS MEDALIST

Public school has always been my fallback from gymnastics. I'm able to go to school during the day and have a place where I don't have to think about gymnastics all the time. It gives me another world that keeps me calm, grounded, and normal.

I DO THE SAME TESTS AND ASSIGNMENTS AS EVERYONE ELSE. I get to school an hour early and take homework with me when I have to travel so that I can keep up. When I'm not traveling, I go to football games and school dances and shop with my friends—ALL THE STUFF ANY OTHER HIGH SCHOOLER DOES.

With my friend, Alice, riding in the homecoming parade. Alice dubbed herself my bodyguard, ha!

At Valley, where I go to high school, they monitor media visits so not many reporters and photographers have been able to come. In fact, when *People* magazine arranged for a photographer to come to school, he thought he'd get to spend a week at Valley. He was only allowed an hour.

"The **WILD CHILD** JUST NEEDED SOMETHING TO DO."

—TERI

EVEN
OUTSIDE THE GYM,
I WAS ALWAYS
ON THE GO.

If I DIDN'T DO GYMNASTICS,

I THINK I WOULD HAVE PICKED DIVING OR TRACK. **Diving** *because it's similar, I guess, to gymnastics.* **TRACK** because I've always *loved running* AND *hurdles.*

I LOVE WRITING POETRY. IT'S A GOOD WAY TO *express my feelings* BECAUSE I CAN'T ALWAYS SAY EXACTLY WHAT **I'M FEELING** WHEN I'M SPEAKING TO THE PUBLIC OR BEING INTERVIEWED. **MY POETRY** IS MOSTLY ABOUT *my experiences,* THOUGH I WRITE ABOUT ANYTHING AND EVERYTHING.

MY PARENTS HAVE ALWAYS MADE SURE I LEAD A *normal life* BECAUSE THEY THINK IT'S IMPORTANT THAT MY LIFE NOT BE COMPLETELY CONSUMED WITH GYMNASTICS. MY MOM AND DAD HAVE ALWAYS WANTED ME TO **SPEND TIME WITH MY FRIENDS** AND DO THE SAME STUFF THAT ANY TEENAGER DOES.

MY CLOSEST FRIENDS ARE A GROUP OF ABOUT 9 OF US WHO HAVE BEEN FRIENDS SINCE KINDERGARTEN. **WE'RE JUST LOUD, CRAZY 16- AND 17-YEAR-OLDS.** AND WE'RE ALL REALLY SUPPORTIVE OF EACH OTHER. THEY'RE SO SPECIAL TO ME BECAUSE THEY DON'T TREAT ME LIKE "SHAWN JOHNSON." THEY COULD CARE LESS WHETHER I'M AN OLYMPIAN OR NOT. WHEN I'M WITH THEM, I'M JUST A NORMAL TEENAGER AND I JUST HAVE FUN.

I'M PROBABLY A LITTLE MORE QUIET THAN MOST OF MY FRIENDS. I THINK IT'S BECAUSE OF HOW **FOCUSED** I HAVE TO BE WITH GYMNASTICS. BUT THAT'S ONE OF THE REASONS I LOVE TO HANG OUT WITH THEM. *They're all really fun and it gives me a sense of the freedom* I DON'T REALLY HAVE WHEN I'M TRAINING.

I'VE NEVER REALLY HAD A BEST FRIEND EXCEPT MY COUSIN, TORI. THAT'S BECAUSE I SPEND SO MUCH TIME TRAINING AND TRAVELING. BUT IN THE LAST COUPLE OF YEARS I'VE BECOME REALLY CLOSE WITH A COUPLE OF MY FRIENDS, SO NOW I FEEL LIKE I HAVE AND CAN BE A BEST FRIEND.

"It doesn't matter how famous she gets or how big the hype gets. She's just a normal teenage girl. She has all the same insecurities they all have."

— Teri

Having fun shopping in Beijing.

3

ROAD TO
gold

I DEFINITELY THINK
SOMETHING HAPPENED
WHEN I FIRST MET
CHOW AND LI.

THEY SAW SOMETHING SPECIAL IN ME. THEY SAW THAT IF I WORKED HARD ENOUGH, I COULD ACHIEVE MY DREAMS.

I TRULY BELIEVE COACH CHOW IS THE PERFECT COACH FOR ME. MY MOM SAYS THAT **I'VE ALWAYS HAD A REALLY PLAYFUL SIDE.** AND COACH CHOW IS OKAY WITH THAT. BEFORE I STARTED AT CHOW'S, THE FIRST PLACE I WENT FOR GYMNASTICS WAS VERY STRICT. MY MOM TELLS ME THAT AT THAT GYM WHEN WE WERE IN LINE, WE WEREN'T ALLOWED TO FIDGET OR GET OUT OF LINE AT ALL. WHEN I STARTED WITH CHOW, MOM SAYS HE LET ME HAVE FUN. **I'D BE OFF DOING CARTWHEELS INSTEAD OF STANDING STILL IN LINE.** MY MOM USED TO TELL COACH CHOW NOT TO LET ME GET AWAY WITH STUFF LIKE THAT, BUT MOM SAYS HE NEVER MINDED. HE ALWAYS KNEW I JUST LOVED TO MOVE.

" I DON'T THINK ANYBODY CAN SEE THAT A 6-YEAR-OLD WILL BE A WORLD AND OLYMPIC CHAMPION. IF SOMEONE SAYS THAT, IT'S NOT THE TRUTH. THEY'RE SUPPOSED TO HAVE A LIFE. IT'S ONLY A LITTLE KID YOU ARE DEALING WITH. "

— COACH CHOW

"Shawn's first meet was in Iowa City at the University. She scored something like a '7' on the vault, **pitiful really, but we were just so happy.** She was just so young and little. When she was waiting to begin her routine, the beam was between Shawn and the judges. She was so tiny she couldn't see over the top of it, so she kept popping up on her tiptoes to see if the judges had signaled her to begin. They were all laughing. **The crowd loved her,** but only because she was so little. Between rotations they'd play songs while everyone was warming up. Shawn would be dancing, waiting in line, having a great time … not a care in the world. They gave ribbons for placement. The worse she did, the more colorful the ribbon. **She didn't care. It was a pretty ribbon.** She was just so excited."

—TERI

I never started gymnastics thinking I wanted to become an Olympian. Gymnastics was always just *my passion* and my **love.**

HERE'S MY BEST ADVICE:

Just Have
FUN

I like to have fun, even when I'm competing. I have fun... **the time of my life.**

"THE RANCH IS WHERE THE WOMEN'S PROGRAM COMES TOGETHER. **THE BAR GETS RAISED HERE.** THE GREATEST LEGENDS HAVE TRAINED HERE; **THE GREATEST TEACHERS** HAVE TAUGHT HERE."

—STEVE PENNY, PRESIDENT OF USA GYMNASTICS

When I'm training, I head to Karolyis' Training Camp in Houston once a month. It's a big ranch where Bela and Martha Karolyi live. In 2005, when I was 13, I made the junior national team and started to make the trip. I stay one week at a time, **leaving behind my parents, friends, and school.** Only Coach Chow gets to come with me. I stay in cabins with three other gymnasts. We sleep in bunk beds. Our roommate assignments rotate. I really love going to Karolyis' Camp. It really **takes me away from all of the distractions.** When I'm there, it's almost nothing except gymnastics. It's hard, long practices, but it's good.

While I'm there, **I'm also able to relax with my gymnastics friends** and calm down. We talk about training, but when we're not training, we do our nails, makeup, and hair. We're on the Internet and listen to music.

Getting ready for Easter at the Karolyi Camp. Bela has eggs for us to color.

AS AN **ELITE GYMNAST,** I SPEND A LOT OF TIME TRAVELING FOR EVENTS. *It's just a totally different environment* TRAVELING OUT OF THE COUNTRY AND GETTING USED TO A DIFFERENT TEAM THAN THE CHOW'S GIRLS I'VE ALWAYS TRAINED WITH. THE TRAINING, THE TRAVEL, AND **THE WHOLE EXPERIENCE CAN BE REALLY HARD.**

I LOVE GYMNASTICS,

BUT IF I HAVE KIDS I DON'T THINK I WANT THEM TO PARTICIPATE IN GYMNASTICS AT AN ELITE LEVEL. *Knowing everything I've gone through as a gymnast,* I'M NOT SURE THAT I COULD WATCH MY KIDS GO THROUGH THAT. **I DEFINITELY WANT THEM TO BE IN SPORTS,** BUT PROBABLY SOME OTHER SPORT.

SHE IS TRULY THE NUMBER 1 GYMNAST IN THE WORLD.

SHE COULD **BLOW ME OUT OF THE WATER.** SOME OF MY TUMBLING MOVES MIGHT HOLD UP A LITTLE. SHE'S DOING HER ROUTINES AT A **FAR HIGHER LEVEL OF DIFFICULTY.**

— MARY LOU RETTON,
1984 OLYMPIC GAMES, GOLD MEDALIST

I'm in this sport to become the next Shawn Johnson. I'm not here to copy or become someone else. I want to be my own person and make history because I'm being me.

SHE'S **READY, SET, GO.** ALWAYS. *When she goes, she goes.* **NOTHING'S HALFWAY.**

—KIM ZMESKAL, U.S. GYMNASTICS CHAMPION 1990–1992,
ABOUT SHAWN TRAINING AT CHOW'S WHEN
SHAWN WAS JUST A KID

My parents have always told me the decision to keep competing in gymnastics is completely mine. But *once I committed myself to becoming the world's top gymnast,* then my parents would remind me that doing my best and being committed to Chow and his training program was **MY RESPONSIBILITY.**

THEY SAID IT WAS A **RESPECT** THING, *and they're right.*

They would never allow me to be disrespectful of Chow and what was expected of me as an elite gymnast. Once I reached that point at an elite level, if I wanted to stick with gymnastics, they made sure I knew I had to follow Chow's rules *out of respect for him, the sport, and the* **COMMITMENT** *I had made.*

S C O R I N G

FOR ARTISTIC GYMNASTICS CHANGED AFTER THE 2004 OLYMPIC GAMES. IT USED TO BE THAT THE HIGHEST SCORE POSSIBLE WAS A PERFECT 10. Now two scores are combined for a final score. ONE PART INDICATES THE DIFFICULTY OF A ROUTINE. THE VALUE FOR THAT PART OF THE SCORE IS DETERMINED BY THE 10 MOST DIFFICULT SKILLS. THE OTHER PART OF THE FINAL SCORE IS FOR EXECUTION. 10 IS STILL PERFECT FOR EXECUTION, AND DEDUCTIONS ARE MADE FOR MISTAKES IN EXECUTION, TECHNIQUE, AND ARTISTRY. BOTH PARTS ARE COMBINED FOR THE SCORE THAT DETERMINES THE OUTCOME OF AN EVENT. Top scores are now typically in the high 15s and 16s. THE NEW SCORING SYSTEM USUALLY MEANS THAT THE MOST DIFFICULT ROUTINES WIN. THERE ARE STILL SOME FANS WHO WANT TO SEE THE ARTISTRY OF THE PAST. But I think most want to see athletes performing skills that have NEVER BEEN SEEN before, taking the sport to the next level. IT WILL BE INTERESTING TO SEE WHO WILL BE ABLE TO HOLD UP PHYSICALLY UNDER THIS SYSTEM AND WHO WON'T.

WHEN I'M COMPETING

I focus on my skills as I go through my routine. My coaches work with me to come up with key words that help me focus on exactly how to perform each skill. THEY'RE SIMPLE THINGS LIKE "STAY UNDER CONTROL," but they help me stay focused. The more I remind myself of those key words and what I need to do, the easier it is. After a while, it's almost like I go into MACHINE MODE.

To **LEARN A NEW ELEMENT,** I start with the basics. **I start with an easy skill that will progress into something bigger.** So to learn a double back, first I learned how to do a single. Once I nailed that, then I worked on the double.

Learning a new skill is really just a lot of **TRIAL AND ERROR.** At Chow's we have a big foam pit that's sort of like a swimming pool filled with foam blocks so that *even if I land on my head, it won't hurt.* I just keep trying until I get it right. **IT TAKES A LOT OF PRACTICE.**

Balance beam is my favorite apparatus because it's so challenging and kinda scary. On the beam you have to work so hard to get a skill. Nothing feels better than when I do a new skill on the beam for the first time.

"WHEN I'm watching Shawn, I take things ONE SECOND AT A TIME. I just go NUMB until it's OVER."

—TERI ON WATCHING SHAWN COMPETE

A CROWD OF 12,490 AT THE WACHOVIA CENTER IN PHILADELPHIA WATCHED US COMPETE AT THE 2008 OLYMPIC TRIALS.

Competing against Nastia really keeps both of us working hard. **I LIKE THE COMPETITION.** I like having one of my good friends be my biggest competitor. **WE PUSH EACH OTHER TO THE**

NEXT LEVEL.

" If SHAWN DID NOT HAVE NASTIA THERE AND IF NASTIA DIDN'T HAVE SHAWN THERE, **NEITHER ONE WOULD HAVE BEEN AS GOOD.** THEY ALSO PUSH THE REST OF THE GIRLS BECAUSE **THEY RAISE THE BAR SO HIGH.** "

— MARTHA KAROLYI, U.S. WOMEN'S NATIONAL TEAM COORDINATOR

It's like we have **2 separate worlds.**

WE HAVE OUR COMPETITIVE-LIKE **ROLE** THAT WE HAVE TO PLAY, and then when we get off the podium and off the mat, **we're friends** and **normal teenagers.**

JUST DAYS BEFORE I *HEADED TO THE* OLYMPIC TRIALS,

MY HOME STATE OF **IOWA** EXPERIENCED

DEVASTATING FLOODS. Volunteers sandbagged Chow's Gymnastics,

but it still had about a **FOOT OF WATER** INSIDE, AND THERE

WERE EVEN FISH SWIMMING through the parking lot. About 100 volunteers

spent 17 hours at Chow's cleaning the gym and building a new floor.

With the Olympic Trials coming up quickly, I had to find a new gym to train in.

But thankfully, I WAS ABLE TO GET BACK IN MY GYM for the last few practices before trials.

THEY WORKED SO HARD TO GET ME THERE.

I wanted to make them proud.

I wanted to be able to take them back TO THEIR HOME COUNTRY AND SHOW THEIR HOME COUNTRY THAT THEY ARE STILL LEGENDS.

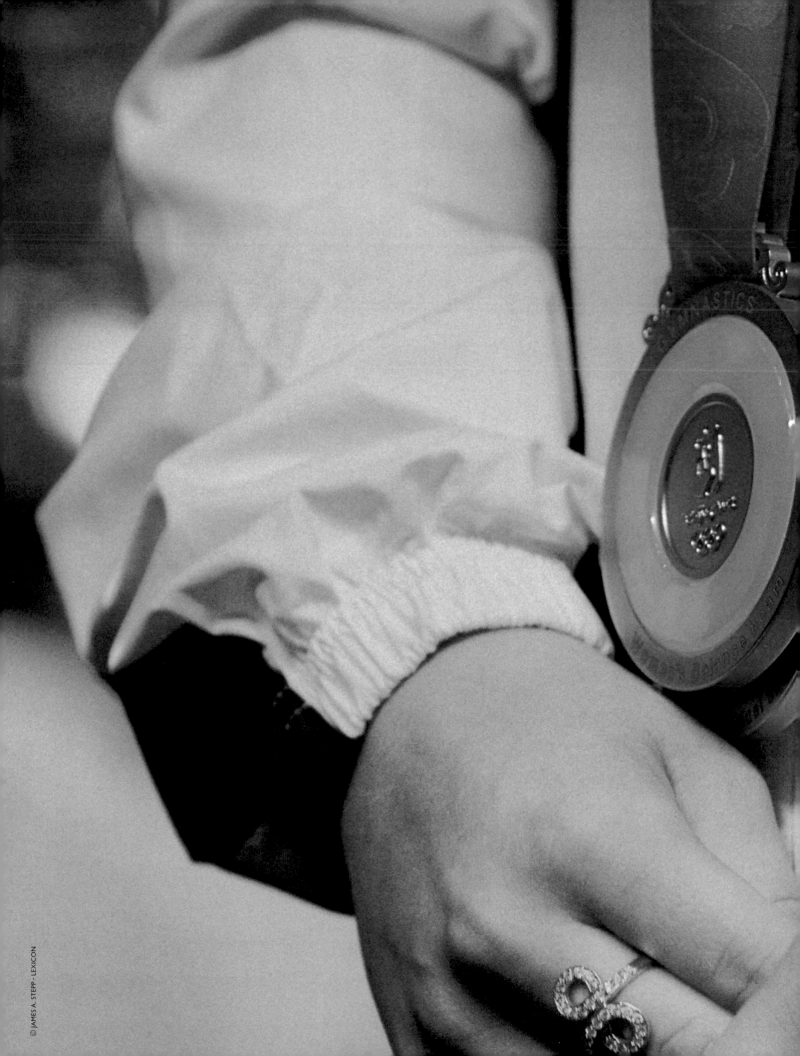

4

OLYMPIC
moment

I brought home **4** medals from Beijing: The three silver medals were for the women's team final, the women's individual all-around final, and the women's floor final events. The *gold medal* was for the balance beam final competition. **I WORKED HARD FOR MY MEDALS, AND I'M PROUD OF EACH AND EVERY ONE OF THEM.** *The medals are beautiful.* Each one has a special design on the front featuring Nike, the Greek goddess of victory, and Panathinaikos Stadium, which was the main stadium of the 1896 Athens games. On the back there's a ring of jade to signify honor and virtue in Chinese culture as well as an engraved emblem of the *Beijing Games.* They're each about **2.75 INCHES** in diameter and a **QUARTER-INCH** thick and weigh approximately **FIVE OUNCES.**

My **parents** and I never took the **Olympics** for granted.

In fact, we never really talked about it with certainty until it actually became a reality for me. I think they discouraged that kind of talk because they thought it sounded arrogant. They didn't want me coming across like a little prima donna—and that was perfectly fine with me.

I think the best way to describe how I felt about making the U.S. *Olympic gymnastics* team is **"scared."** I mean, the experience was overwhelming—I was going into the *biggest meet of my life* and I wanted to represent my country as best I could. But at the same time, it also felt amazing to know that I earned that spot on the team and that **I proved I was the person people had been talking about.**

OLYMPIC MOMENT

060

I am very good friends with the Chinese team. *We have just always had a great relationship.* Of course, there is the communication barrier, but you can tell through body language and through the few words that we do know that we care about each other and we want the best for each other. I think that has to do a lot with Chow. Right before the Olympics, Chow and Li gave me a special Chinese name: "Golden Flower." It was a great honor. When we visited the Forbidden City, the Emperor's nephew painted my Chinese name for me.

Proudly holding my four medals at my homecoming event in Des Moines.

Finally in Beijing! Holding the Olympic torch.

The Emperor's nephew presenting my parents with the a "Golden Flower" painting.

With my friends on the Chinese Olympic team.

"It was a great EXPERIENCE. I can't find a better way to go back to Beijing than as **HEAD COACH** of the OLYMPIC team. It was an honor."

—Coach Chow

I gave my HEART and SOUL to everything at the OLYMPIC GAMES. There wasn't any more I could give. When you train your whole life to get to the Games, *you train for gold*. But honestly, a silver around my neck three times means more to me than ANYTHING.

We respect China for what they've done. They had a great meet and they really brought their game. I honestly think our team did great. We overcame so many obstacles. We're proud of each other no matter what we do. We're still a family, still a team. In the end, we're more than happy and proud to represent the USA wearing silver around our necks.

The same goes for the all-around competition. Nastia and I were both going for the gold — you don't go for silver. But coming in second to Nastia is easier than coming in second to a different country. Whether Nastia won or I won, it's great because it's the USA winning. Whether she came in first or I came in first, it didn't matter. We wanted to see USA on top.

My individual scores for the team competition were **16.000** on the vault, **16.175** on the balance beam, **15.100** for my floor routine, and **15.350** on the uneven bars. *The final score?* China: 188.900, **USA**: **186.525**.

> "SHE **PROVED** THAT SHE CAN DO THE **BALANCE BEAM.** She showed the world and the judges that, after battles with the scores, she could keep FIGHTING and FIGHTING and get the gold. I'm so *proud of her.*" —COACH CHOW

© JERRY LAI · U.S. PRESSWIRE

© MARK J. REBILAS · U.S. PRESSWIRE

I WANTED TO MAKE CHOW *proud, and I feel like I did.*

After my routine, I could tell by the way that he hugged me and by the look on his face that **HE WAS MORE PROUD OF ME THAN HE HAS EVER BEEN.** During warm-ups for my final event, the balance beam,

I WASN'T FEELING QUITE RIGHT. I had a headache and a queasy stomach, and I *fell each of the first seven times I practiced my routine.* At that point Chow told me I needed to wake up. **AND I DID.**

Performing my beam routine. I didn't think too hard about it. I just went out and did it.

I earned a **16.225** to win the gold.

© MARK J REBILAS - U.S. PRESSWIRE

Finish*ing* off *my* first **Olympic Games**

by earning the *gold medal* on my last routine was, to me, the best ending I could have asked for. I've never felt so proud and relieved.

I want to hold on to that feeling forever.

COURTESY ERIN DELAHANTY COURTESY ERIN DELAHANTY COURTESY ERIN DELAHANTY

Exactly the truth came out, who had the NERVE, the PREPARATION, who can STAY on the apparatus! The best ones are ours! Yes! Yes! Yes!

—BELA KAROLYI,
U.S. WOMEN'S NATIONAL TEAM COACH

"She is **ROCK-SOLID**. She has the ability to do her best at the moment it's most IMPORTANT."
—Martha Karolyi

"She has an extremely big **explosiveness** and the joy of performing. **She makes it look easy** to perform in front of large audiences in pressure situations. *That takes some maturity.* —BELA KAROLYI"

I liked the *Olympic Village*. **It was a place where we could relate to the other athletes and hear their stories.**

Winning 4 medals

wasn't the only rewarding aspect of **my Olympic experience** in Beijing. I also enjoyed spending time in the *Olympic Village* and getting to know the other athletes. **16,000** athletes from around the world stayed there, and it was cool to experience different cultures.

Once my events were over, I got to spend time with my *PARENTS* and have a *mini-vacation* in China —something I'm *NOT* used to!

WE WENT TO THE **GREAT WALL** AND I GOT TO BE A

I ALWAYS HAVE FUN WHEREVER I GO, BUT THIS WAS EVEN

TOURIST FOR A FEW DAYS, WHICH WAS *REALLY GREAT.*

MORE SPECIAL TO ME BECAUSE I WAS REALLY ABLE TO **RELAX.**

My gymnastics events took place during the first half of the GAMES, and I could have gone home when they were over. I decided to stay because I knew it would probably be my only time in China.

It was great being there, especially because I HAD SO MANY GREAT SUPPORTERS. It was crazy to go out on the streets and have people run toward me, asking for autographs and pictures. It was definitely an honor, but a unique one at that.

I also had the opportunity to go on a Chinese game show, which was kind of like Letterman. I had cheerleaders dancing around me and gifts galore. Then, I got to imprint my hand in a GOLD STAR for the show's wall of fame. It was so much fun!

I wanted to stay for the Closing Ceremony because it's part of the whole OLYMPIC experience, and I

I'M SO GLAD I STAYED.

The Closing Ceremony was *amazing*. It was the perfect *ending* to a perfect Olympic **EXPERIENCE.**

wanted to finish it off RIGHT.

The whole *production* was unbelievable. Getting to **spend time** with all the athletes from all the different sports was wonderful— I GOT TO RELAX AND ENJOY MYSELF.

5

IN 1 THE
spotlight

I don't know if *anything*

WILL GO BACK TO THE WAY IT WAS

I don't know that I **EVER** want it to.

I feel like **this is what** I've **WORKED** for.

Vince Vaughn was really nice. When I went to ask if I could take a picture with him, he knew who I was!

It was so fun to meet Mario Lopez. I love Saved by the Bell!

This is me and Zac Efron from High School Musical.

Happy to be with fellow gymnasts Shannon Miller, Blaine Wilson, and Dominique Dawes.

With Meredith Vieira, co-host of The Today Show.

It's *definitely* hard to **control**

DISTRACTIONS.

But it comes with the sport. WOMEN'S GYMNASTICS gets a lot of attention, but *that's also why we love it:* People *recognize* our hard work.

I met **Al Gore** at the Democratic National Convention.

Me and **will.i.am**.

With John Legend backstage before the **Democratic National Convention**.

Sheryl Crow **and me**.

I got to meet Daren Kagasoff on the set of **The Secret Life of an American Teenager**.

Shaking hands with Stevie Wonder.

Here I am in BEIJING —more than **6,000** miles from home— and I found COCA-COLA, right in front of the *Basketball* venue. It's so great to find a piece of home, EVEN ON THE OTHER SIDE OF THE WORLD!

Being on TV is awesome,
BUT SOMETIMES IT MAKES ME A LITTLE NERVOUS TOO.

When I'm sitting next to Bob Costas, David Letterman, Jay Leno, or Ellen, I get *nervous* about what to say, and try to guess what they're going to ask me next. *I guess I'm starstruck.*

I USUALLY DON'T WATCH THE BROADCASTS LATER ON BECAUSE I'M EMBARRASSED.

PHOTOS COURTESY *LATE NIGHT WITH DAVID LETTERMAN*

I ALWAYS FIND STUFF WRONG, AND I TEND TO LOOK FOR THE IMPERFECTIONS.

PHOTOS COURTESY *THE ELLEN SHOW*

WHEN I WAS ON ELLEN, Ellen brought up the subject of **marriage proposals.**

That's because sometimes when I look up into the crowd I see guys with signs that say, "*Marry me, Shawn.*" **And one time there was even this guy who was saying,** "*Call me.*" How was I supposed to do that?

" *One guy had 'I love Shawn'* painted on his chest. **I HAD TO GET A PICTURE,** so I told him to stand up. After I took the picture, I told him, '*I'm Shawn's dad.* NOW SIT BACK DOWN.' "
—DOUG

I 've been lucky to be a part of several special events this year. I was asked to lead the *Pledge of Allegiance* at the **2008 Democratic National Convention** in **Denver** the night that Barack Obama gave his acceptance speech.

I also attended the **Teen Choice Awards** in August 2008, where I won *Choice Female Athlete*. I was up against amazing athletes—**Candace Parker, Danica Patrick, Serena Williams, and Maria Sharapova**—so winning was a huge honor. I was the first gymnast nominated for the award, making the win even more special.

FROSTED P♪NK
WITH A *twist*

I'VE PARTICIPATED IN THE
Frosted Pink
Series for the past **TWO** years.

© ROBERT BENSON - WIRE IMAGE

It's the anchor event of a MULTI-YEAR TELEVISION NETWORK, CABLE NETWORK, AND MULTIMEDIA CAMPAIGN that focuses on educating viewers about cancers that primarily affect women. I got to collaborate with some wonderful women, including **Mary Lou Retton** and **Shannon Miller.**

This year SHARON OSBOURNE accepted the Nationwide® Insurance Woman of Courage Award, and CYNDI LAUPER and other singers were involved, too.

The fight against cancer is an issue that's especially close to my family, because one of my grandmothers beat the disease.

IT'S SUCH AN HONOR

to know that I have little kids looking up to me the way I look up to other athletes.

Knowing that I'm an ACTUAL INFLUENCE on them is the greatest reward and feeling I've ever had. But it can definitely be scary, too, because it makes me think, "If I was going to do this, would I want them to do it, too?"

HONO

I enjoy using my role model status in a positive way. I'm part of a campaign sponsored by the Ad Council, the Department of Health and Human Services, qubo, the U.S. Olympic Committee, and NBC that encourages children to control their food portions, exercise, and maintain a healthy energy balance. That's because I believe it's important for kids to understand that they don't need to be an Olympian to be healthy. It can be as easy and as fun as getting up to play for an hour a day and keeping an eye on the amount and type of food you eat.

There are definitely times when I wonder whether I've done the right thing or if I should have taken a different road, such as when I'm going through hard practices or hard training times—WHEN SOMETHING DOESN'T GO PERFECTLY. During these times I don't always feel the GREATEST about myself, and I rethink everything I've done.

BUT IT'S THOSE DOUBTS THAT ACTUALLY MAKE ME APPRECIATE EVERYTHING I'VE DONE.

Once I have a great competition or a great practice, or I see a little girl on the street who says "I wanna be like you" or something like that, **that really makes me appreciate everything I've done.**

IOWA IS THE BEST PLACE EVER.

I was born, raised, and still live in the great state of IOWA. I'm an IOWA girl at *heart* and always will be.

It's the *most* **SUPPORTIV** and caring place.

You know you have *people to go home to* who will be a part of you.

© LEXICON

COURTESY ALISSA CUNNINGHAM

© JAMES A. STEPP • LEXICON

© JAMES A. STEPP • LEXICON

CONGRATULATION

Iowa's Golden Girl 2008

Accepting a special plaque that declares SHAWN JOHNSON MONTH in Polk County.

Iowa Governor Chet Culver declared October 17 "Shawn Johnson Day" in Iowa.

A local sculptor carved a butter statue of me for the 2008 Iowa State Fair.

There's a life-size bronze statue of me in the Iowa Hall of Pride. The statue weighs as much as 41,000 pennies.

A banner decorated the Wells Fargo Arena in Des Moines for my homecoming celebration.

SOMETIMES PEOPLE CAN BE **HURTFUL**— BUT THAT'S JUST PART OF LIFE.

I try not to let other people's opinions get to me. Some of the best advice my mother ever gave me was to never let what others say be the truth. Let them say what they want to say, but DON'T LET IT BECOME REALITY. That way, I don't have to feel bad about anything. It's their problem, not mine.

When I returned from Beijing, **8,000** people showed up at the Wells Fargo Arena in *Des Moines* to welcome me home. I couldn't believe that many people would gather to see me—**it was crazy!**

WHEN I FIRST SAW THE CROWD ON CAMERA while waiting behind stage, I thought I was watching the **Democratic National Convention.** *It was the best welcome home ever—I loved every minute of it.*

I'm **thankful** to have such supportive fans.

I still can't believe all these people came out to welcome me home—but **I'm so glad they did!**

The Nadas, a local band, performed. They even dedicated a welcome home song to me.

©JAMES A. STEPP - LEXICON

© LEXICON

"It's nice that there are so many people who appreciate what I love.
—TERI

PHOTOS © JAMES A. STEPP - LEXICON

One of the best parts of the event? I got to shoot T-shirts into the audience.

My mom and dad, catching a glimpse of the huge crowd for the first time.

THIS IS CRAZY. *WHY WOULD YOU COME OUT HERE FOR ME?*

—SHAWN, AFTER SEEING THE
HUGE CROWD GATHERED FOR HER
HOMECOMING CELEBRATION

210

108